JIU JITSU

The Official World Jiu Jitsu
Federation Training Manual
Blue Belt to Brown Belt

Professor Robert Clark 9th Dan

First published 1993 by
A & C Black (Publishers) Ltd
35 Bedford Row, London WC1R 4JH

ISBN 0 7136 3720 X

A CIP catalogue record for this book
is available from the British Library.

Acknowledgements
All photographs by Sylvio Dokov.

Printed in Great Britain by
Redwood Press Limited, Melksham, Wiltshire

Contents

Foreword

This is the second of my three books on jiu jitsu practice. The first covered the novice grades from beginner to Green Belt of jiu jitsu. This covers the intermediate grades, taking you from Blue Belt through to Brown in the World Jiu Jitsu Federation system. Though this book is of value to any martial artist with an enquiring mind, it is indispensable to the World Jiu Jitsu Federation member who will want to supplement his training with a step-by-step analysis of each and every technique.

I am assuming that readers will have looked at the first book and so will be aware of how to prepare for training. They will also know the basic stances used in jiu jitsu, so I am not obliged to describe them over again.

Not only stances, but many of the techniques described here are discussed in the first book. By combining those earlier instructions with the expanded applications mentioned now, you will obtain a greater insight into their use. I therefore strongly recommend that you read and revise the White/Green Belt Syllabus (also published by A & C Black, 1991).

Putting the art into martial art

Before launching into the present syllabus, I would like to devote a few lines to the practice of jiu jitsu. The first thing I want to say is that jiu jitsu is a martial art. We generally understand 'art' to mean some form of creative skill, the exercise of which transforms the mere execution of technique into something greater. What that something is, I cannot define. I suppose it is a fusion of consummate technical skill with a mental approach that changes each technique into a movement of beauty and power. Let me try to illustrate what I mean by reference to some of the advanced forms that you will encounter when you enter the higher dan grade ranks.

It is possible to go through any one of these forms in a perfectly adequate if mechanical way. The performer executes each movement perfectly, though with a detached expression – a clinical coldness or precision. Compare this with a performance in which the jiu jitsuka lives the form, injecting a vitality and enthusiasm that is missing from the first display. In the hands of the latter performer, the form becomes alive.

Well, that is the target I want you to aim for. First of all, master technique through constant repetition. The more you practise a move, the less you will need to think about how it is done. And the less you have to think about how it is done, the more you can put into doing it. First learn the technique – then learn the art!

So, never say, 'Well, I've got that – now what's next?'. You can never *master* an art; all you can do is learn to give an ever better expression of that art.

With that in mind, let's now go on and look at the techniques needed to take you from Purple Belt all the way through Blue to Brown Belt.

Robert Clark

Blue Belt Syllabus

Loin or hip wheel

Fig. 1 Face the opponent with your left foot and fist both leading. Bend your knees slightly and make ready to move. The opponent faces you in the same stance.

Fig. 2 The opponent thrusts his right hand forwards in either a punch or an attempt to grab hold of you. Twist your hips strongly to the left and allow your left foot to slide forwards and turn outwards, so it lies just inside the opponent's left foot. Deflect the opponent's right arm with the palm of your left hand, curling the fingers around his upper arm. Note the position of your right guarding hand at this point!

Fig. 3 Spin quickly around, maintaining your grip on the opponent's right arm and securing a new grip under his right armpit. Step through with your right foot and bend your knees, so your centre of gravity drops below that of the opponent. Your feet are quite close together.

Fig. 4 Straighten your knees and lift the opponent off his feet. Then draw him forwards with your left hand whilst pushing him with your right. This tips the opponent over your back and onto the floor in front of you. Keep hold of his right arm with your right hand, so he can't roll away from you. Kneel into the opponent's ribs and head.

Fig. 5 Bend the opponent's right elbow and wrist, applying a double-handed grip to the back of his hand. This is one of the classic holds of jiu jitsu, and one which you must be able to apply from a variety of throws – not just from loin or hip wheel! It is not a new technique; you will have practised it for your White Belt (*see* fig. 39 on page 31 of my first book).

Three ways of escaping from head chancery

Technique 1

Fig. 6 Head chancery is where the opponent holds your head against his side by folding his arm around it. In the first example, the opponent stands in front of you, holding your head against his right ribs with his right arm. In some versions of this hold, his left arm may loop under your right armpit, thereby trapping your arm as well as your head. But it doesn't matter which he does – just reach quickly forwards and attack the muscles on the back of his legs with the tips of your fingers. This causes the opponent to ease his hold whilst uncontrollably thrusting his hips forwards.

Fig. 7 Swing your right forearm up and into the opponent's groin. This causes him to release the hold still further.

Fig. 8 Reach up with your left hand and take the opponent's elbow. At the same time, take his wrist with your right hand. Draw down with your left hand and push with the right.

Fig. 9 Straighten the opponent's arm, then step through with your left foot. Bring your right foot sharply around until you are facing in the same direction as the opponent.

Fig. 10 Transfer your weight forwards and onto your left foot whilst moving your left hand around until it pushes on the back of the opponent's shoulder. Lift the opponent's arm until it is vertical and press down on the bent wrist. You will recognise this lock as another from the White Belt Syllabus (*see* fig. 33 on page 28 of my first book).

Technique 2

Fig. 11 The second escape from head chancery is made from the more usual side-holding position. Sharply strike the opponent's thigh with right hammer fist.

Fig. 12 Use this distraction to step quickly through with your left foot. At the same time, take the opponent's right elbow in your right hand and bend your left elbow ready to use the flat of your hand.

Fig. 13 Drop onto your right knee, so your centre of gravity drops well below the opponent's. Push the inside of the opponent's left knee whilst pulling strongly on his right elbow.

Fig. 14 As a result of the drawing action of your right hand and the lifting action of your left, the opponent falls forwards over your back.

Fig. 15 Keep hold of the opponent's right arm as he topples onto his back in front of you. Then apply a lock (*see* the earlier syllabuses and also the later ones in this book for options!).

Technique 3

Fig. 16 The third and final escape from head chancery also begins from the side-on position. Strike just above the opponent's right knee with hammer fist.

Fig. 17 Step quickly through with your left foot, so it comes across the front of the opponent's. At the same time, drop your right hand down and take the front of the opponent's right upper ankle. Thrust your right hand upwards and press against his upper back.

Fig. 18 Pull on the opponent's right foot whilst pressing against his back with your right palm. His left foot is trapped by yours, so he falls forwards onto his face.

Fig. 19 Fold the opponent's left foot over his right and press against them with your left knee as you secure his foot with your left hand.

Four countermeasures against garrotting

Technique 1

Fig. 20 The opponent faces you and winds his belt around your neck, crossing it in front of your Adam's apple.

Fig. 21 Slide your right foot forwards and strike the opponent's mid-section with a double palm heel.

Fig. 22 Step up to your right foot, turning your body until you are sideways-on to the opponent. Draw down on his right elbow and push up his left.

Fig. 23 Step diagonally right across the front of the opponent with your right foot. This prevents him from moving his right foot forwards.

Fig. 24 Pull with your left hand and push with your right as you overbalance the opponent across your right leg. Keep hold of his right arm and he will fall onto his back in front of you. Punch him in the temple to complete the sequence.

Technique 2

Fig. 25 Begin the second sequence in the same way as the first, but this time step out to the left with your left foot whilst using a palm heel thrust against the opponent's nose to drive his head back. At the same time, strike the opponent in the ribs with a left palm heel.

Fig. 26 Pull down on the opponent's right elbow whilst pushing upwards under his left armpit.

Fig. 27 Bring your right foot through and hook back against the opponent's right leg. This, plus the combination draw and push on his arms, will topple him backwards. Keep hold of his right arm as he falls, and he won't be able to roll away from you. Apply an armlock to complete the sequence.

Technique 3

Fig. 28 This time the garrotte is applied from behind.

Fig. 29 Step forwards with your right foot and turn around quickly in an anti-clockwise direction, so your left foot leads. Strike the opponent's ribs with a left back fist.

Fig. 30 Bar the opponent's upper leg with your left forearm and take his left calf in your right hand.

Fig. 31 Jerk his foot forwards and up with your right hand whilst pushing back with your left. This causes the opponent to fall onto his back. Keep hold of his right leg with your right hand and drop the left palm down onto his knee. Then apply a finishing technique, the ideal one to use being found in the Green Belt Syllabus on pages 98 and 99 of my first book.

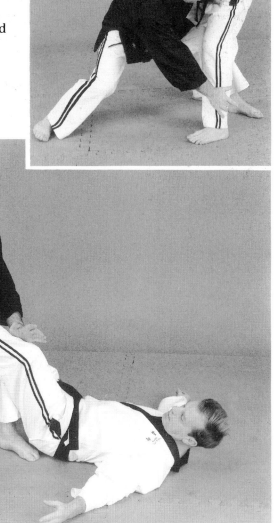

Technique 4

Fig. 32 Again the garrotte has been applied from behind. Step forwards with your right foot, turn anti-clockwise and knock the opponent's arms upwards with your left forearm. At the same time punch him in the solar plexus with your right fist.

Fig. 33 Lean forwards and grab the backs of the opponent's knees.

Fig. 34 Straighten up and the opponent will fall onto his back in front of you. Hold on to his legs and kick him in the groin.

Variations on holding down

Revise the earlier hold-down techniques to be found in the White, Yellow and Green Belt Syllabus. Apply whichever hold down best suits the circumstances of any particular throw.

Technique 1

Fig. 35 We encountered this hold down earlier in the syllabus, and noted that it first appears in fig. 39 on page 31 of my first book. The opponent is pinned down by your body weight bearing down on him through your knees. His wrist and elbow are folded and a double-handed grip is applied to the back of his right hand.

Technique 2

Fig. 36 In this hold down, your left arm has entangled the opponent's right arm. Your left arm lies over the top of his upper arm, and dips under his forearm. Secure the hold by pressing against his elbow with your right palm.

Technique 3

Fig. 37 Here you have thrown the opponent onto his back, whilst keeping hold of his right arm with your left. Step over the opponent's head with your right foot and hook your instep under his left upper arm. Bend your knees and raise the opponent's head whilst taking his straightened right arm back and across your left thigh in a straight armlock. Apply pressure to the opponent's neck by judiciously straightening your right knee. Beware: this technique is extremely dangerous!

23

Technique 4

Fig. 38 Once again you have thrown the opponent onto his back. Grip his wrist with both hands and step forwards and over his head with your left foot. Draw the opponent onto his left side.

Fig. 39 Drop to your knees, trapping the opponent's left arm under your right, and squeezing his throat between the back of your thigh and calf muscles. Draw back his right arm and lock it against your right upper thigh.

Technique 5

Fig. 40 This is substantially the same as the previous hold down except that both your hands have shifted to the back of the opponent's hand.

Technique 6

Fig. 41 This hold down has many features in common with the one shown on page 137 of the **Green Belt Syllabus** (*see* figs 274-7). You have thrown the opponent and turned him half on his face by drawing on his right arm. Step on his left forearm to aid in this action. Take the opponent's right arm in a double grip, the thumbs pressing into the back of his hand.

CONTINUED

Fig. 42 Step forwards and over his arm with your left foot and push his arm against the back of your knee. This frees the left, so it can function as a guarding hand.

Fig. 43 Drop onto your right knee.

Fig. 44 Lean forwards to trap the opponent's arm against your body and draw your right foot back.

Fig. 45 Lower your weight onto your left buttock, entangling the opponent's right arm between thigh and stomach. Push the opponent's face into the mat and strike him in the back of the neck.

CONTINUED

27

Fig. 46 Lean across him and drop your left hand to the mat.

Fig. 47 Scoop under the opponent's left elbow with your left arm, pressing against the back of his shoulder in a second entangled armlock.

Technique 7

Fig. 48 Here the opponent has been thrown onto his face in front of you (*see* again fig. 18). Take up his wrists and step forwards with your right foot.

CONTINUED

Fig. 49 Kneel down, trapping the opponent's right arm behind your right knee.

Fig. 50 Draw your left foot in and work your instep behind the opponent's head. Push the opponent's left arm against the back of your left knee and apply a wristlock.

Technique 8

Fig. 51 In this technique you have followed the opponent down to the mat. He is lying on his back and you have dropped onto your right hip, trapping his right arm beneath you. Reach across his chest and work your right arm under his left upper arm. Then take his wrist. Press against his throat with the edge of your left hand.

Fig. 52 Pull the opponent's left fist close to his head. Then work your right arm under his head. Take hold of his left upper arm with your left and lever his head up.

Technique 9

Fig. 53 In this technique, you have taken the opponent's right arm in a straight arm lever across your right thigh. Slide your right arm under the opponent's head and hook his left upper arm. Rearing back will lever the opponent's head forwards. Take care – this is a dangerous technique!

Technique 10

Fig. 54 In this, the last of the hold downs studied here, the opponent has tried to force your head back with his right hand. Draw your head back and push the opponent's arm across his body. Then encircle his neck with your right arm, take your right wrist with your left hand and grip tightly. Lower your head and spread your legs wide for maximum stability.

Breaking strangles and chokes on the ground

Revise the section entitled 'Breaking ground strangles' in the Yellow Belt Syllabus (*see* pages 84–91) before going on to practise these techniques.

Technique 1

Fig. 55 The opponent kneels between your legs and applies a strangle.

Fig. 56 Strike the opponent a glancing blow across the side of his jaw with your left palm. At the same time, take his right wrist with your hand and draw your right knee up, so the sole of your foot presses against his left knee.

CONTINUED

Fig. 57 Push his left knee and turn his right hand palm upwards as he falls diagonally forwards. Raise your left foot.

Fig. 58 Slide your left foot under the opponent's chin, pressing the sole down on his left forearm. Apply a lock to the opponent's right wrist.

Technique 2

Fig. 59 This time the opponent is kneeling to the side of you as he applies the strangle. Strike him a glancing blow across his chin with the palm of your left hand.

Fig. 60 Push his head to the side with your right palm and bring your right knee up.

Fig. 61 Swing your left leg up and trap the opponent's jaw behind your knee.

Fig. 62 Use your left leg to force the opponent down onto his back. At the same time, draw his right arm against your thigh and lever it back. You must be close to the opponent for this to work correctly.

Technique 3

Fig. 63 The opponent kneels between your legs to apply the strangle. Reach out and hook back with both heels, striking the opponent in his kidneys. Press the back of your left hand against the opponent's right elbow and take his left elbow with your right hand.

Fig. 64 Twine your legs around the opponent's and twist strongly to your left. At the same time, push his right elbow out and lift his left elbow.

Fig. 65 Bring your left arm around the back of the opponent's neck and take his upper arm in a strong grip.

Fig. 66 Roll onto your left side and strike the opponent in the ribs with hammer fist. Your left arm prevents him from using his left to counter attack.

Fig. 67 Continue rolling until you are on the top and bring your right arm across the opponent's throat. Secure the hold by gripping your left upper arm in your right hand. Bear down on the opponent's throat.

Technique 4

Fig. 68 The opponent kneels astride you. Bring your left arm up and take it behind the opponent's upper left arm.

Fig. 69 Take your left fist in your right hand and press hard against the opponent's left elbow. This turns him sideways-on.

Fig. 70 Twist strongly to the left and topple him.

Fig. 71 Guard your face with your left hand and punch the opponent in the groin.

Technique 5

Fig. 72 Reach up with both hands as the opponent kneels astride you.

Fig. 73 Pinch the flesh of his chest as you seize his lapels.

Fig. 74 Arch your body and throw the opponent forwards.

Fig. 75 Roll the opponent onto his back and strike him with right hammer fist, back fist or knife hand. Protect your face as you do so!

43

Technique 6

Fig. 76 Here the opponent kneels in front of your shoulders to apply the strangle.

Fig. 77 Force his elbows outwards in order to bring his head down. Then take his ears in both hands and knee him in the head.

Fig. 78 Roll him onto his back and finish him with a hammer fist to the jaw.

Technique 7

Fig. 79 The opponent is once more kneeling between your legs. Bring your left hand through and press against his right elbow with your forearm.

Fig. 80 Bring your left knee over the opponent's right arm and hook his chin with your instep. Push his left hand free with your right.

Fig. 81 Roll onto your left hip and extend your right foot.

Fig. 82 Continue rolling onto your left knee, keeping hold of the opponent's right wrist as you do so.

Dropping version of body drop

Fig. 83 Face the opponent with your left foot leading. The opponent attempts to punch you with his right fist. Step quickly forwards with your right foot, placing your foot mid way between his feet. Block his punch with your right forearm and hold your left hand in a guard position.

Fig. 84 The opponent then tries to punch with his left fist. As he does so, secure his right arm with your left and block his second punch with right knife hand.

Fig. 85 Turn anti-clockwise, drawing your left foot up and kneeling down. Slide your right foot in front of the opponent's right ankle. Draw down and forwards on his right arm whilst pushing up his left. The effect of this combination is to tumble him onto his back in front of you.

Fig. 86 Keep hold of the opponent's right wrist, levering it across your left thigh whilst driving a palm heel into the side of his head.

Fig. 87 Slide your right arm under the opponent's head and lever it up. Note that the opponent's left arm is immobilised by the position of your hand. His right arm is trapped by the position of your knee.

Scissors and naked choke hold

Fig. 88 Face the opponent in left stance. The opponent steps quickly forwards with his right foot and attempts to punch you in the chest. Step to the side with your left foot and deflect his punch with your right hand. Hold the left ready in a guard position.

Fig. 89 Push the opponent's right arm, encouraging him to spin around and attempt to use left back fist or hammer fist. Stop his attempt with your left palm. Note that his back is now fully turned to you.

Fig. 90 Strike him in the kidneys with both fists.

CONTINUED

51

Fig. 91 Swing your right arm around his throat, drawing him backwards.

Fig. 92 Bring him down to a sitting position on the mat.

Fig. 93 Sit down, roll back and wrap your legs around his mid section, securing the scissors by hooking your ankles together. Roll right back and continue to apply the choke.

Spring hip throw

Fig. 94 Turn into the opponent's reverse punch, blocking his right arm with your left. Note the position of your right guarding hand.

Fig. 95 Keeping your grip on the opponent's right elbow, step quickly through with your right leg. At the same time, slide your right arm under the opponent's armpit and around his back. Bend your knee to drop under his centre of gravity and bump his right foot free of the mat.

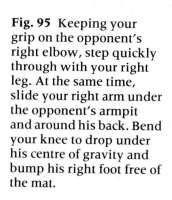

Fig. 96 Lean well forwards and draw him over your right hip.

Fig. 97 Complete the technique with a punch to the opponent's head. A one-knuckle punch is extremely effective when used to attack the vital point behind the opponent's ear.

Scooping throws (back and front)

Technique 1

Fig. 98 The opponent attempts to club you with his right fist. Shift your weight backwards slightly and deflect the blow with rising block.

Fig. 99 Immediately transfer your weight forwards and bring the little finger edge of your hand glancing across the front of the opponent's throat. Note the position of your guarding right hand.

Fig. 100 Keep your left hand in position and thrust your right hand between the opponent's legs.

Fig. 101 Lift the opponent with your right hand as you push him backwards with the left. This topples him backwards onto his shoulders. Complete the technique with a punch to the groin or face.

Technique 2

Fig. 102 Deflect the opponent's hammer fist, this time using an x-block.

Fig. 103 Bring your right knee sharply into the opponent's chest – don't allow him to move away from you!

Fig. 104 Drop your right hand onto the back of the opponent's neck and drive your left between his legs.

Fig. 105 Lift with your left arm and push down with your right so the opponent is thrown forwards onto his face.

CONTINUED

Fig. 106 Drop onto your right knee and strike the opponent's groin with right hammer fist.

Fig. 107 Follow up by taking the opponent's left ankle in your right hand and drawing it back against his buttock.

Fig. 108 Use your left hand to fold the opponent's right leg back and over the top of his left.

Fig. 109 Secure the lock by stepping over the opponent's legs with your left and jamming them with your left thigh. Maintain your hold on the opponent's right foot. Complete the technique by striking the back of the opponent's head.

Indian death lock

Revise figs 243–7 of the Green Belt Syllabus (*see* pages 123–5 of my first book) before attempting this technique.

Fig. 110 Having just thrown the opponent onto his back, drop onto your right knee and strike him in the groin with right hammer fist. Note the position of your left guarding hand.

Fig. 111 Drop your left hand and take hold of the opponent's left shin. Lean forwards and quickly thrust your right hand under the opponent's right knee.

Fig. 112 Lift the opponent's right knee, so his foot is drawn back towards his buttock. At the same time, slide his left foot across the front of the right.

Fig. 113 Secure the hold by taking the opponent's left ankle in your right hand. Transfer weight to your left hand and bring your right knee up. Thrust the sole of your right foot into the underside of the opponent's jaw.

Downward/inside forearm block

Fig. 114 Face the opponent in left stance, with your left guard hand leading. The opponent punches with his right fist. Move your left fist down in a sharp circular movement that brings the little finger edge into contact with the opponent's forearm. Note the hip action that turns your body partly away.

Fig. 115 The opponent next punches with his left fist. Turn your hips to the left and knock his punch outwards with the little finger edge of your right fist.

Roundhouse kick to solar plexus executed whilst walking

Fig. 116 The opponent approaches you from the left side.

Fig. 117 Turn your hips to the left, sliding out your right foot and blocking the opponent's punch with the edge of your left hand or forearm.

CONTINUED

Fig. 118 Bring your right knee up until it points at the target.

Fig. 119 Kick the opponent in the solar plexus with the ball of your foot. Pull your toes back to avoid injury.

Sleeper hold from head chancery

Technique 1

Fig. 120 Block the opponent's right punch with your left forearm, hooking your fingers over his elbow.

Fig. 121 Draw your right arm back and swing it forwards, so that the forearm strikes the opponent quite hard across the side of his neck. Step forwards with your right foot as you do this and draw the opponent's right arm towards you.

Fig. 122 Allow your right elbow to fold around the opponent's head and link your hands, trapping his right arm against your ribs.

Technique 2

Fig. 123 Turn strongly into the opponent's punch and block it with your right forearm.

Fig. 124 Drive your right fist upwards, snagging the opponent's jaw with your elbow.

Fig. 125 Fold your elbow and bring your forearm around the back of the opponent's neck. Bring your left hand up ready to link with the right.

Fig. 126 Link your fingers and drop onto your right knee, turning your hips to the left. The opponent's neck is trapped against your arm and shoulder.

Outside forearm block/elbow to ribs

Fig. 127 Step diagonally forwards and to the left as the opponent punches with his right fist. Deflect his punch with your right hand.

Fig. 128 Step forwards with your right foot and drive your elbow into the opponent's ribs.

Fig. 129 Twist your hips to the left and strike the opponent's kidneys with back fist or hammer fist.

Purple Belt Syllabus

Valley drop throw

Fig. 130 Begin from left stance, turning your hips anti-clockwise as you block the opponent's punch with your left hand. Note the guarding position of your right hand.

Fig. 131 Step to your left foot, so both feet come together. Insert your right hand under the opponent's armpit.

CONTINUED

Fig. 132 Bend your knees and roll back onto your backside at a 45° angle whilst drawing the opponent with your left hand and lifting him with the right. The opponent will be overbalanced forwards, toppling over you to land head first on the mat. Keep hold of him and be prepared to execute a follow-up lock or hold as appropriate.

Fig. 133 This is how an early stage of the above throw looks from the other side.

Counter to straight armlock

Technique 1

Fig. 134 The opponent has trapped your right arm and is applying a straight arm lever against it (revise figs 41–3 on page 32–3 of the White Belt Syllabus in my first book).

Fig. 135 Use the palm of your left hand to push the opponent's left elbow forwards.

CONTINUED

Fig. 136 Rotate your forearm until it
faces palm downwards – this defeats
the lock.

Fig. 137 Step across the front of the opponent's feet with your right leg and bend your knees, so your waist drops below his centre of gravity.

Fig. 138 Straighten your knees and lift the opponent's feet clear of the mat, then draw him over your right hip so he falls onto his back in front of you. Finish the technique with a lock or hold.

Technique 2

Fig. 139 Begin as before, sliding your right leg behind the opponent's as you push his left elbow forwards.

Fig. 140 Topple the opponent backwards over your right leg, rolling back with him as he falls. Drop your left hand onto the opponent's left knee. Apply a strike or lock/ hold to complete the sequence.

Fig. 141 This is what the throw looks like from the other side.

Counter to back arm and collar hold

Technique 1

Fig. 142 The opponent takes the back of your collar in his left hand and jams your right arm up your back with his right.

Fig. 143 Step forwards with your right leg and twist your hips. Take hold of the opponent's right wrist and strike into his mid section with a left back fist.

Fig. 144 Transfer your body weight forwards and raise your left arm over the opponent's head.

Fig. 145 Trap both of the opponent's arms inside your left.

Fig. 146 Draw your right foot up and around, bending your knees and turning your back towards the opponent. Slip your right arm around his back.

Fig. 147 Straighten your knees, lifting and drawing the opponent over your right hip.

Technique 2

Fig. 148 Begin as before, but this time step diagonally forwards and to the right with your right leg, so the opponent is drawn forwards. Strike him in the ribs with back fist.

Fig. 149 Twist sharply to the right as you step back and strike him in the jaw with your right elbow.

Fig. 150 Raise his right arm and fold his wrist.

Fig. 151 Take his right arm backwards and insert your left under his elbow, locking the little finger edge against the side of his hand in a figure-four grip.

Fig. 152 Twist your hips to the left, draw in your left foot and bend both knees. Pull the opponent over your back and straighten your knees to lift him from the mat.

Fig. 153 Topple him over your right hip onto his back. Keep hold of his right wrist!

Technique 3

Fig. 154 Begin as before by stepping forwards with your right foot, turning your hips and striking the opponent's ribs with back fist.

Fig. 155 Drop your left hand sharply in time to stop the opponent's attempted knee strike.

Fig. 156 Slide your left foot to the outside of the opponent's and duck under his arm.

Fig. 157 Straighten up and take the opponent's right wrist in your right hand.

Fig. 158 Fold the opponent's elbow with your right hand and force your left under his elbow. Take your right wrist in your left hand. This conveniently brings his head into knee strike range.

Fig. 159 Take the opponent down onto his face. Retain your hold on his right hand, applying leverage by leaning forwards with your left forearm whilst pressing with your thigh. Push his head down with your right hand.

Counter to bar choke

Technique 1

Fig. 160 The opponent stands in front and to your left, holding your collar with his left hand and applying a choke with his right wrist.

Fig. 161 Slide your left foot between the opponent's legs and strike him in the ribs with back fist. Note the guarding position of your right hand.

Fig. 162 Take his right wrist in your right hand and fold the wrist. Slide forwards with your left leg and push your left palm against his elbow. This takes his head down.

Fig. 163 Lean forwards over the trapped arm and apply the hold. Keep the opponent close to your side in order to control him effectively.

Technique 2

Fig. 164 Begin from the same opening position. Turn and slide your left foot behind the opponent's right. At the same time, lift the opponent's left elbow with your right hand as you draw down on his right elbow.

Fig. 165 Hook back with your right heel into the back of the opponent's leg.

Fig. 166 The opponent falls backwards over his trapped right leg and lands on his back in front of you. Keep hold of his right wrist! Kneel into the opponent's back and head, taking his straight arm back across your right knee.

Roundhouse kick to kidneys

Fig. 167 Block with your left hand as the opponent punches and step to the right with your left foot to set up the correct angle for the kick. Note the position of your right guarding hand.

Fig. 168 Bring your right knee up and around until it points at the opponent's ribs, then snap the ball of your foot into his kidneys. Pull back your toes to avoid hurting them. Quickly retrieve the kicking foot and set it down.

Upward and rising block

Fig. 169 The opponent attacks with his right fist. Deflect it by taking your right forearm diagonally forwards and up.

Practise a series of upward/rising blocks, one after the other.

Upward inside forearm block

Fig. 170 Turn your hips and bring your left fist upwards and outwards into the attacker's wrist. The action of your forearm is something like a windscreen wiper.

Fig. 171 Pull back your left fist and perform a second block with your right to the opponent's following punch. Repeat the blocks with alternate arms.

Downward inside forearm block followed by punch

Fig. 172 Deflect the opponent's punch with the little finger edge of your left fist. Your arm describes a circular movement and knocks his punch outwards.

Fig. 173 Continue the circular movement and slide around with your left leg. Put your right hand on the opponent's shoulder to control him. The opponent's forearm is trapped against your shoulder as you press down on his shoulder with your left hand, using the right to follow with a punch.

Front kick followed by side kick

Fig. 174 Deflect the opponent's punch with your left hand and bring your right knee forwards and up. Use the ball of your foot to snap kick the opponent in the groin. Note the position of your right guarding hand.

Fig. 175 Partly retrieve the right foot and turn away from the opponent. Deflect with your right hand and use the left to guard your face.

Fig. 176 Thrust the heel and little toe edge of your foot into the opponent's knee. Retrieve the spent kick afterwards.

Vary this technique by performing front kick, as before, and then kicking to the side at an imaginary second opponent.

Full shoulder

Before attempting this technique, revise the shoulder throw which you studied as part of your Green Belt Syllabus (*see* fig. 314 on page 152 of my first book).

Technique 1

Fig. 177 The opponent takes hold of your lapel with his right hand.

Fig. 178 The opponent attempts to punch you with his left fist. Deflect it with your right hand.

Fig. 179 Spin quickly around and take his left fist across his chest.

Fig. 180 Slide your right leg diagonally back and across the front of the opponent and move your shoulder under his right upper arm. Turn the opponent's left arm palm upwards and pull it towards you.

Fig. 181 Lean well forwards and bump the opponent over your back, throwing him onto the mat in front of you.

Technique 2

Revise shoulder throw again from the Green Belt Syllabus, this time looking at fig. 315 on page 152 of my first book.

Fig. 182 Here the opponent has attempted to punch you with his right fist. Block it with your left hand and guard your face with your right.

Fig. 183 Lift the opponent's right arm and step quickly under it, turning your back on him. Slide your right foot out behind you and extend your right arm forwards.

Fig. 184 Bring the opponent's right arm down across your shoulder and drive your right elbow back into his ribs.

Fig. 185 Then thrust your right arm up and under the opponent's upper arm to act as a fulcrum. Bear down on his right wrist with your left hand and bump him up and over your back.

Head, hip and knee moves

Before trying the following technique, revise figs 279–81 of the Green Belt Syllabus in my first book (*see* pages 138–9).

Fig. 186 Block the opponent's punch with your left hand, guarding your face with your right.

Fig. 187 Draw the opponent's arm down, turn your hips and strike the side of his head with your right forearm.

Fig. 188 Step right through with your right foot, so it bars across the front of the opponent's. Curl your right arm around the back of the opponent's neck.

Fig. 189 Sink down on your right knee and draw the opponent forwards and over your back.

Side thrust kick

Fig. 190 Step out with your left foot and deflect the opponent's punch with your right hand.

Fig. 191 Lift your right knee and thrust the sole of your foot into the opponent's ribs.

Also perform this kick by stepping to the other side and kicking with your left foot. Kick to the opponent's knee, mid section or face.

Front snap kick

Fig. 192 Take the opponent's punch with your left hand and raise your right knee until it points at the target. Then snap the lower leg out in a fast arc. Pull back your toes and strike with the ball of the foot.

Use this technique to attack the opponent's groin, solar plexus or chin. Practise delivering the kick with both front and rear legs.

Wedge block

In this sequence, wedge block has been combined with a defensive sweeping loin throw. Revise the throw by referring to figs 211–15 of the Green Belt Syllabus in my first book (*see* pages 108–9).

Fig. 193 The opponent takes you in a double lapel grasp. Step back with your right foot and bring both hands up between the opponent's arms. Push outwards against his elbows. Wedge block prevents the opponent from head-butting you.

Fig. 194 Snap kick the opponent in the solar plexus with your right foot. Your hands take hold of his upper arms.

Fig. 195 Drop the spent kick in a forward position and turn your hips until your back is presented to the opponent. Pull the opponent's right arm and push up on his left.

Fig. 196 Sweep back strongly with your right foot, bumping the opponent into the air.

103

Shoulder wheel

Fig. 197 Block the opponent's punch with your left hand whilst placing your left foot mid way between his feet.

Fig. 198 Step quickly through in an anti-clockwise direction, ducking under the opponent's raised right arm. Reach down across the front of the opponent's shin with your right arm.

Fig. 199 Straighten your knees and lift the opponent bodily. Lift up with your right arm whilst drawing the opponent's right arm across your chest. This creates a see-saw effect and rolls the opponent over your shoulders and onto his back at your feet.

Brown Belt Syllabus

Winding throws (inside and outside)

Technique 1

Fig. 200 The opponent attempts to punch you with his right fist. Block with your left hand and guard with the right as you slide your leading left foot across in front of you. Step through with your right foot and strike the opponent a glancing blow across his chin with palm heel. Retain your grip on his right elbow.

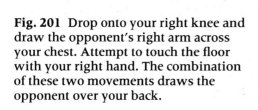

Fig. 201 Drop onto your right knee and draw the opponent's right arm across your chest. Attempt to touch the floor with your right hand. The combination of these two movements draws the opponent over your back.

Fig. 202 Retain your grip of the opponent's arm and bring your right arm around and behind his head.

Fig. 203 Force the opponent's head forwards and place the palm of your right hand to the mat just inside his upper arm. Lean back to apply the lock.

This technique is known as 'outer winding throw'.

Technique 2

Fig. 204 Block the opponent's punch with your left hand and take his elbow. Guard your face with the right and slide your left leading foot into the middle. Step around and through as before, but this time thrust your right hand under the opponent's right arm. Bend your knees until you are below his centre of gravity.

Fig. 205 Drop onto your right knee and draw the opponent's right arm downwards. Try to touch the floor with your right hand.

Fig. 206 Keep hold of the opponent's right wrist and draw his arm out straight. Slip your right arm under his and press down against the side of his jaw and throat. Use your own right elbow as the fulcrum and apply leverage to the opponent's elbow.

This technique is known as 'inner winding throw'.

Variations on leg sweeps

Fig. 207 A classic sweeping technique begins with a left hand deflection of the opponent's punch as you step across with your left leg.

Fig. 208 Step through and around with your right leg into a transitional position. Both knees are bent and your right arm has slipped around the opponent's back.

Fig. 209 Swing your right leg forwards . . .

Fig. 210 . . . then swing it back into the opponent's shin as you simultaneously draw him forwards across your right hip.

You can sweep the opponent's leg at various heights, from ankle to thigh. Try them all!

111

Fig. 211 Apply the sweep from a side-by-side position, this time taking the opponent's right ankle as you draw his body weight back and over it. Vary the height of the sweeping leg.

Fig. 212 Repeat the previous technique, but this time attempt to sweep both legs.

Rolling ankle

Technique 1

Fig. 214 Sit down on your left buttock, drawing the opponent forwards and off balance. Bar his right leg with your shin.

Fig. 213 Block the opponent's punch with your left hand and guard with the right – but apart from turning it outwards slightly, don't move your leading left leg! Slip your right hand under the opponent's left armpit and step across with your right foot, so it comes to the outside of the opponent's right ankle.

Fig. 215 Continue the rolling action, throwing the opponent clear by extending your right leg.

Technique 2

Fig. 216 Begin as for the previous technique but this time put your right foot to the side of the opponent's left ankle and grip the back of his neck with your right hand.

Fig. 217 Roll back exactly as before and extend your right leg to help spring the opponent over you.

Corner throw

Fig. 218 Begin as for the previous two techniques, blocking the opponent's punch with your left hand and guarding with the right hand. Then step inside the opponent's left ankle with your right foot.

Fig. 219 Place your right foot to the outside of the opponent's right and then sit down, drawing him forwards and off balance. His feet are barred by your shins, so he is forced to fall forwards. Use both legs to help spring him over.

Rear throw

Technique 1

Fig. 220 This technique is applied when the opponent stands in front of you.

Fig. 221 Step forwards with your right foot and draw the left up after it. Take the back of the opponent's neck with your left hand and place your right palm against his stomach.

Fig. 222 Sit down and roll back, at the same time pulling with your left hand and pushing with the right. This draws the opponent forwards and off balance, so he rolls over the top of you.

Fig. 223 The throw is completed with the opponent on his back and you resting on your left hip. Keep hold of his wrist and draw back your right foot for a kick.

Technique 2

Fig. 224 This throw is applied in response to the opponent's punch. Stop his right punch with your left arm and his left follow-up with your right.

Fig. 225 Step forwards smartly with your right foot until both your feet come near together, slightly to the opponent's right. Then place your right palm on the opponent's stomach and roll back, executing the throw as before.

Cross ankle throw

Fig. 226 Block the opponent's right punch with your left hand and stop his left punch with your right. Step across with your left leg.

Fig. 227 Step through with your right foot, so it bars the opponent's right ankle. Draw down strongly with your left hand and push up with the right, so the opponent is unbalanced over your right leg.

Leg wheel

Fig. 228 Approach the opponent from behind and take his left hand forwards with your left. Your right arm encircles his back. Note the position of your left foot.

Fig. 229 The opponent takes hold of your belt in his right hand. Step through with your right leg.

Fig. 230 Drop your right foot so that it bars the front of the opponent's right ankle. The opponent's arms are now hopelessly crossed. Sweep back with your right foot and tumble the opponent forwards and onto his back.

Outer wheel

Fig. 231 The opponent punches with his right fist. Block it with your left hand, curling the fingers over his elbow. Then he punches with his left fist. Stop this with your right hand, at the same time twisting your left foot until it points outwards.

Fig. 232 Step through with your right foot, bringing your bodies close together. Swing your right foot forwards and draw/push the opponent's shoulders back and downwards.

Fig. 233 Swing your right leg back, striking both of the opponent's legs and bumping him into the air.

121

Action against three or more attackers

This part of the syllabus shows your ability to think tactically whilst on the move. Select three partners to work with and station them so that one faces you and the other two stand one either side of you. Begin with slow techniques that you can cope with, then increase the speed of your responses as you get the knack of it.

For example, the opponent facing you steps forwards to punch. You block the punch and counter with a front kick. Withdraw the spent foot and set it down at your side. Then block and side kick the opponent on your right side before turning to deal with the one on your left. Block him and counter with a third kick. This is a fairly simple sequence in that the responses are relatively undemanding.

The object is to be dealing with one opponent whilst being aware of the others: as you complete one response, you are setting up the second. Note that the opponents come at you one after the other, and not simultaneously.

As you become more skilled, you will be able to incorporate throws into your responses. Whenever you do this, always try to throw your opponent at such an angle that he impedes another's attack. This is an example of tactical thinking.

Variations on stomach techniques

Fig. 234 The opponent attempts to push you with both hands.

Fig. 235 Take the opponent's upper arm in your left hand and his lapel in your right. Step back with your right foot and draw him forwards.

CONTINUED

Fig. 236 Roll back and place your foot in the opponent's stomach. Turn your head to the side. Provided the rolling action was vigorous enough, the opponent will be drawn forwards, picked up on your foot and thrown onto his back.

Fig. 237 You can vary this throw by using both feet to lift and spring the opponent over.

Fig. 238 You can also apply the throw from a sideways-on position, taking the opponent's right arm in your right hand and his right ankle in your left.

Outer hook throw

Fig. 239 The opponent faces you, with his left foot leading. Step forwards with your right foot, placing it to the outside of the opponent's left ankle. Take his left guarding hand in your left hand and block his punch with your right. Note how your foot is twined around the back of his.

Fig. 240 Thrust your right arm across the front of the opponent's throat, driving his head back. This overbalances him over your right knee.

Fig. 241 Keep hold of the opponent's wrist as he falls and apply a follow-up technique as appropriate.

Several ways of throwing opponents from behind

Not all throws need be performed whilst facing the opponent. Sometimes your block will spin him in such a way that his back faces you. The following selection looks at just some of the throws which can be applied when you are standing behind an opponent.

Fig. 242 Step forwards and take the opponent's hair in your right hand. Jerk his head back, raise your right knee and drive the sole of your foot into the back of his knee. Pull his head down at the same time and he will fall onto his back.

Fig. 243 The second of these techniques also employs a kick to the back of the opponent's knee. This time, you have dropped on your left side to the mat. Hook your left leg around the opponent's right ankle and kick into the back of his knee.

Fig. 244 For the third of these techniques, slide your right foot between the opponent's feet so that it bars his right shin. Lean forwards and take his left shin in your left hand. Reach up and place your right hand against his left shoulder. Pull and lift his ankle with your left hand whilst pushing down on his shoulder with the right hand.

Fig. 245 The fourth technique begins with you sliding your right foot between the opponent's feet as you kneel down. Your right ankle is now barring his right shin. Take the opponent's left shin in your right hand and jar him so that he falls forwards.

Fig. 246 Perhaps the most obvious of these techniques is simply to reach down and take the opponent's ankles with both hands. Use your shoulder to jar him forwards whilst drawing his ankles back. This will drop him onto his face in front of you.

Fig. 247 Keep hold of his ankles, then step through and drop your heel onto the back of his neck.

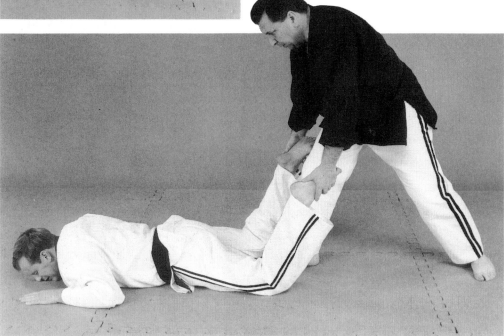

This is a starting position for many groundwork techniques, some of which will be encountered next.

Shoulder dislocations

Technique 1

Fig. 248 This technique follows on directly from fig. 247 on the previous page. Lean forwards and pick up the opponent's arms. Draw them both straight up and step through with your right foot. Sufficient leverage will dislocate both shoulders.

Technique 2

Fig. 249 Release the opponent's right arm and bring your right foot across to the left side of his head. Sit down on his left shoulder blade and draw his left arm upwards, using both arms to apply a strong leverage.

Technique 3

Fig. 250 This technique also follows on from fig. 247. This time take up the opponent's arms and step forwards so your left foot is near his left armpit.

Fig. 251 Jam the opponent's left arm against the front of your left thigh. Bring the opponent's right arm up his back.

Fig. 252 Hold the opponent's left wrist in your left hand and jam his arm in position by pressing down on his back.

Fig. 253 Now turn your attention to his left arm, lifting it off your left thigh and folding it forwards.

CONTINUED

Fig. 254 Slide your left hand forwards and press down on the opponent's back, jamming his left arm. Lean well forwards.

Fig. 255 Drop to your knees and use your thighs to lift the opponent's elbows. Withdraw your hands and place them just below the opponent's elbows. Lift his elbows to apply leverage.

Dropping version of reverse body drop

Fig. 256 Slide forwards with your left leg and block the opponent's punch with your left hand. Take his right elbow, bringing your right forearm up and across the side of his neck.

Fig. 257 Step through with your right foot and pull the opponent backwards by drawing on his right arm and pulling on his neck.

Fig. 258 Drop onto your left knee and slide your right foot behind the opponent's left ankle. Draw the opponent over your right leg, so he falls onto his back. Then apply a strike or hold as appropriate.

Shoulder crash

Fig. 259 Stop the opponent's punch with your left hand and guard your face with the right. Slide your leading left foot across.

Fig. 260 Pull the opponent's right arm straight with your left, step through and duck under it. Slide your right hand between the opponent's thighs and take the back of his leg.

Fig. 261 Straighten your knees and lift the opponent, balancing him across your shoulders. Then either lean forwards and throw him to the floor in front of you, or throw him backwards, so he lands behind you.

To minimise the force of being thrown from such a height, your partner should take a firm hold of your belt with his right hand.

Palm heel knockout blow to chin

We have encountered palm heel strike several times in this and earlier syllabuses. Now it is time to look at it in detail. Palm heel strikes the opponent with the pad of flesh at the bottom of the palm. The fingers are brought together and slightly curled, and the thumb is pressed against the side of the hand. There are various ways of using palm heel of which the following is a selection.

Fig. 262 Block the opponent's punch with your left hand and turn your hips square-on. Transfer your body weight forwards and swing your right palm heel forwards and up, so that it clips the opponent's jaw and knocks his head back.

Fig. 263 This time, turn your body sideways-on to the opponent and use the blocking hand in a horizontal, glancing palm heel strike that rotates the opponent's head.

Practise the upward travelling and the horizontal palm strike as a one-two combination.

Fig. 264 You can also use a double palm heel that drives the opponent's head back sharply.

Fig. 265 Use double palm heel to attack widely separated targets simultaneously.

Left upward block with knife hand to neck

You first practised knife hand at the very beginning of your jiu jitsu training. Revise the technique by looking at fig. 27 of the White Belt Syllabus (*see* page 25).

Fig. 266 *Above* Deflect the opponent's punch with a rising block that takes it well clear of your face.

Fig. 267 *Above right* In the interests of clarity, both this and the next photograph have been taken from the opposite side. Following the block, transfer your body weight over your rear right foot, fetching your open right hand back to your ear as though saluting.

Fig. 268 *Right* Transfer the weight over your front leg, draw the opponent's right arm forwards and down, and strike him across the side of his neck with the little finger edge of your right hand. Note that your hand rotates into a palm-upwards configuration just before impact.

Back kick when held by both hands from behind

Fig. 269 The opponent takes hold of both of your wrists from behind. Step forwards with your left foot.

Fig. 270 Lift your right knee . . .

Fig. 271 . . . and thrust the heel directly back into the opponent's mid section.

Practise the kick on both legs, then use it as the first part of a combination that continues as follows.

Fig. 272 Drop the spent foot between the opponent's feet and lift your arms away from the sides of your body.

Fig. 273 Draw the opponent's hands together and smack your right palm heel into the fingers of his left hand to loosen his grip.

Fig. 274 Take the opponent's left hand in your right, driving your thumb into the underside of his wrist. Then peel it from your left wrist. Lift his forearm and duck under it as you step back with your right leg. Be prepared to use your left hand to block the opponent's right-handed punch.

Fig. 275 Take the opponent's right forearm in your left hand, release your grip on the opponent's left wrist and wrap your arm around the opponent's back. Slide your right foot out so it bars both of the opponent's feet and throw him over your right hip.

Roundhouse kick to solar plexus

Fig. 276 Slide your leading left foot to the left and block the opponent's punch with your right hand.

Fig. 277 Maintain your guard as you bring the right knee forwards and up. Then snap the foot out and strike the opponent in the solar plexus with the ball of your foot. Pull your toes back to avoid injuring them.

Side kick to kneecap (using side of foot)

Begin as for fig. 276 on the previous page.

Fig. 278 Raise your right knee and bring it across the front of your body. Then thrust the little toe edge of your foot diagonally downwards and into the side of the opponent's knee, allowing your supporting foot to swivel outwards.

Upward kick to kneecap (using heel)

The opponent punches with his right fist and you respond by transferring your body weight over your back leg, so the stance shortens. Deflect the punch with your left hand.

Fig. 279 Keep hold of the opponent's spent punch and swing your right leg forwards and up, so the heel catches his kneecap with an upward-glancing movement.

It is also possible to use this kick from a partially sideways-on position by swivelling on the supporting leg to give the technique a roundhouse kick-like action.

Three different blocks all using same blocking arm

The opponent stands with his left foot forwards and performs three punches, one after the other.

Fig. 280 The opponent first punches with his right fist. Block this by swinging your left arm up in a windscreen wiper-like movement that knocks the punch outwards. The block is executed using the thumb side of the wrist and forearm.

Fig. 281 Then the opponent punches with his left fist, withdrawing the right as he does so. Take your left arm straight across your body and knock the opponent's punch outwards. This time the block is executed with the little finger side of the wrist and forearm.

Fig. 282 The opponent punches again with his right fist, this time aiming at your stomach. Bring your left arm smartly downwards and across your lower body, deflecting the punch with the little finger side of your wrist and forearm.

This, of course, is not the only sequence of three blocks using the same arm. You might also use the sequence head block/cross block/lower block. All these alternatives are valid.

Attacking back of legs

This is a résumé of all the techniques you have already practised which involve rear sweeping movements – inner and outer hock throws, kicks, etc.

Arm and shoulder throw with shoulder lock and wristlock

Fig. 283 Slide your left leading foot diagonally forwards and block the opponent's punch with your right hand.

Fig. 284 Step through with your left foot and take the opponent's spent punch down and to your right. Take the back of the opponent's left wrist in your right hand and apply a wristlock by flexing the joint as far as it will go. Lift the right arm, ensuring that the elbow is straight, and apply pressure to his right shoulder blade with your left hand.

Fig. 285 Maintain pressure on the opponent's arm and slide your left foot across the front of your right.

Fig. 286 Then sit down and lean back, thereby lifting the opponent's arm as you press down against his shoulder.

Chop to neck with side kick to solar plexus delivered to two opponents

In the interests of clarity, the second opponent has been left out.

Fig. 287 Draw down the opponent's punch and take your right hand back to your right ear – as though saluting.

Fig. 288 Turn your hips towards the opponent and strike him on the side of his neck with knife hand.

Fig. 289 Your hips are now turned away from the second opponent, whose back would be to the camera and who would be set up for a side kick. Lift your right foot from the mat and thrust it into the imaginary second opponent's solar plexus.

Roundhouse kick from ground to lower body

It is not always possible to perform kicks from a well set up stance. The object of this exercise is to practise your roundhouse kick after having been thrown, or having fallen, to the mat.

Fig. 290 You are lying on your left side with your left knee forward and the right trailing. Your hands are in a defensive guard position.

Fig. 291 Bring your foot up smartly in a roundhouse kick into the opponent's groin or pit of the stomach. Then be prepared to perform a follow-up technique.

Side thrust kick to back of knee from ground

Here the opponent has in effect stepped past you, leaving his rear right leg within range of your technique.

Fig. 292 Hook your left instep around the opponent's ankle, thereby preventing him from drawing it forwards. Then thrust the sole of your right foot into the back of his right knee (*see also* fig. 243 of this syllabus).

Side snap kick

Fig. 293 Slide your leading left foot to the left in order to avoid the opponent's right punch. Block his arm with your right hand and grip his elbow. Raise your right foot and snap your right heel into the side of his knee. Then execute an appropriate follow-up.

The difference between side thrust kick and side snap kick lies not in the form of the techniques, but in the way they are executed. Thrust kick uses the sole of the foot and attempts to penetrate the target. By comparison, the snap kick explodes on the surface of the target.

Side thrust kick to kneecap/roundhouse kick to ribs

Fig. 294 Transfer the weight to your back leg and block the opponent's right fist with your left hand. Guard your face with the right hand. Turn sideways-on to the opponent and raise your left knee. Lean away and thrust your foot into the opponent's leading left kneecap.

Fig. 295 Withdraw the spent kick, twist your hips back and set your left foot down with the toes turned outwards. This sets up your right hip for the following kick.

Fig. 296 Pivot on your left foot and kick the opponent in the ribs with the ball of your foot. Draw back your toes to avoid injuring them.

155

One-handed throws

The following selection is designed to get you started.

Technique 1

Fig. 297 Tuck your left hand into your belt. Turn your hips and deflect the opponent's right punch with your right hand.

Fig. 298 Hook your arm around the opponent's neck and drop onto your left knee, shooting the right across and in front of his. Draw him forwards, so he overbalances over your right leg.

Technique 2

Fig. 299 Begin as for fig. 297 on the previous page, but immediately after you block, slide your right foot between the opponent's feet and attack his neck with knife hand. Your hand twists palm-downwards on impact.

Fig. 300 Hook your right arm under the opponent's and take hold of it. Turn your hips until your back faces him, drawing your feet together and bending your knees. Straighten your knees and throw the opponent.

Technique 3

Fig. 301 Step diagonally forwards and block the opponent's right punch with your right hand.

Fig. 302 Step between the opponent's feet with your right foot. Turn your hips away and drop to your right knee. Reach down and curl your right forearm around the back of the opponent's right leg. Jar the opponent's upper leg, so he falls backwards.

Fig. 303 Keep hold of the opponent's right leg, so he doesn't roll away from you. Complete the technique with a back fist to the opponent's ribs.

Getting ready to teach others

By the time you have reached Brown Belt, you will have attained quite a respectable level of skill. Many advanced students gain a great deal of further insight into their own practice by teaching others. This is because explaining a technique to other students demands that you look at that technique in an analytic way, and analysis of this kind leads to a greater knowledge about the technique itself.

So, not only is teaching rewarding from the point of view of seeing others progress, it is also beneficial for our own practice. Whether or not you are interested in eventually becoming a fully qualified WJJF Coach, you should seek some teaching experience through your club.

Typically, the club coach will ask you to assist him by supervising a group of lower grade students. Make sure he explains fully what he wants you to do, then do that and no more!

According to whether you feel at ease teaching others, and whether you have a talent for passing on your skill (some high grades do not have this talent!), then your club coach may enrol you in a WJJF Assistant Coach course. This is usually a single day course held at the WJJF Headquarters in Fazakerley, Liverpool.

All the elementary 'do's' and 'don'ts' of teaching will be explained and then you will have the chance to coach a group of your fellow candidates. A friendly and useful discussion afterwards will indicate areas of improvement. Successful candidates receive a coaching certificate and record book.

Whether or not you are interested in making both a lucrative and rewarding career from coaching, do enrol on one of the WJJF's courses.

For further details, contact:

The World Jiu Jitsu Federation
Barlows Lane
Fazakerley
Liverpool L9 9EH

Tel: 051 523 9611.

Index